T0197093

I Am America

WILLIAM FOWLER

authorHOUSE®

AuthorHouse™
1663 Liberty Drive
Bloomington, IN 47403
www.authorhouse.com
Phone: 1 (800) 839-8640

Published by AuthorHouse 01/30/2018

ISBN: 978-1-5462-2684-0 (sc)
ISBN: 978-1-5462-2682-6 (hc)
ISBN: 978-1-5462-2683-3 (e)

Library of Congress Control Number: 2018901309

Print information available on the last page.

Any people depicted in stock imagery provided by Thinkstock are models,
and such images are being used for illustrative purposes only.
Certain stock imagery © Thinkstock.

This book is printed on acid-free paper.

This book is dedicated to Heather, Sarah, William and Joshua.

Divorce

You live on a beautiful island,
Surrounded by love and beauty.
Suddenly,
You are banished.
You cross a wooden bridge
To the mainland,
The only bridge to the island.
The mainland is full of strangers,
Judgmental and critical.
You turn around and see
That the bridge is burning.

Life Is A Mystery To Me

Life is a mystery to me.
People searching,
Searching eternally.
Seeking out the answers,
Looking for the questions.
Which ones are the right ones for me?

Interior Design

It's your world.
You create it.
Imagination becomes reality.
From nothing comes something.
Colors dark and bright,
Lighting for the night,
Textures hard and soft.
Wood. Metal. Paint. Fabric.
It's your world.
You live in it.
Own it.

Absence

Some say that absence makes you fonder.
I say it causes eyes to wander.

Haiku Haiku

Four or five of them.
Then seven more syllables.
Then five more of them.

The Internet

It's called the internet.
It's called the web world wide.
In case you do forget,
Man's knowledge at your side.

Info rides the silent air,
And streams in rays of light.
It's like a big world's fair,
All day and all the night.

You buy and sell and talk,
And read and write and view.
Tread lightly where you walk,
Be careful what you do.

You don't know who's watching.
Be careful what you say.
All can see your botching,
Forever and a day.

It brings us together.
It tears us far apart.
Beware of human nature,
The evil in our hearts.

Cars

Majestic moveable monuments,
Of proud American steel.
Gas guzzling behemoths.
Road cruisers.
Highway boats.

Oh, you cars of the 50's and 60's,
I remember you.
I recall the awe and the wonder.
Each September would bring
A new school year,
New clothes for school,
A new TV season,
But I looked forward for different reasons.
For in car dealerships,
Soon would appear,
The polished new models
Of a new model year.
School was okay,
And clothes were all right,
But oh, those new cars...
What a beautiful sight.

When I was five,
I stood out in the yard.
A man came along and we talked about cars.
He asked me,
"What's this one, and that one, and that?"
I had all the answers.
I had them down pat.
He looked at me with marvel and awe.

Something was going on in his craw.
My mom came outside,
And I started to fidget.
He said, "Ma'am, he's either a genius or midget!"

When I was fifteen an ad on TV
Spoke of the Auto Show in New York City.
I asked my father, and we both went.
As we walked from display to display,
We had a great time.
We spent half a day.
What more
Could an adolescent boy ask for?
Cars – foreign, domestic, exotic and normal.
Beautiful spokesmodels in gowns oh, so formal.
Women and cars.
I reached for the stars.
The year after that I started to dream.
I had a plan, I had a scheme.
I'd walk into a parking lot,
And drive away in the car I got.
When I awoke so happy I'd feel.
I knew in a year that dream would be real.

Oh, you cars of the 50's and 60's.
I remember you.
With your grilled faces of steel,
And your bulbous taillights.
Taking me to places so real,
very day and every night.
I'm glad I learned how to drive.
It made me feel so much alive.

Oh, you cars of the 50's and 60's,
I remember you.

They don't make them like you anymore.
They all look alike, these days,
Except for Lambos, Ferraris and Vettes.
Boxy or curvy, they share the highway.
It used to be so simple then,
The make and model in words,
On the rear, front or sides.
Now Kia, Honda, Acura, Infiniti, Toyota, Nissan
Hide behind symbols,
In this day and age of political correctness
And climate concern.

Oh, you cars of the 50's and 60's,
I remember you,
And I remember the days of my youth.

The Family

We gather here, from near and far,
To share a dream and catch a star.
To share our love of letters and words,
Of nouns and adjectives and verbs,
Of sounds and pause, and rhythm and rhyme,
Poetic, prosaic, in three quarter time.
Of thoughts unspoken, yet spoken loud,
We share our work, of which we're proud.
It's him, it's her, it's you, it's me.
Together we're a family.

1956 Buick Special

My father bought you new,
Three weeks before I arrived.
A new car, a new child,
A family.
You are the first car I recall,
Two tone white and blue.

I sat in my dad's lap,
And held the steering wheel.
We drove you down the road.
The dream was real.
When new cars were inexpensive,
And life was simple.

You had a new paint job,
Back in 1962.
I waited every day
To see you.
All white and smelling of new paint.
Old becoming new.

A child could swim in you,
Or get lost inside of you.
My father traded you in,
In 1962.
For a brand new
Chevy II.

1966 Buick LeSabre

My father bought you new.
You were Verde Green,
Which is funny,
Because verde is green in Spanish.
So you were green green.

The week that you arrived
We went to Boston.
My first long trip.
A new car smell.
Towns with funny names,
In a state called Massachusetts.

My father traded you in,
And showed up at my school,
In a brand new Chevy Impala,
Four years later.

1967 Ford Mustang

My father bought you used,
In 1971.
You were one of my favorite cars.
I learned how to drive in you.
It made me feel alive and true.

Outside black and red interior.
I drove you and I felt superior.
Envied then, a classic now.
I wish I still had you.

My father traded you away,
In 1974.
My mother was upset.
You weren't the car
I drove anymore.

Muse

I use it as my muse,
To write the words that I choose.
With license poetic,
I write frenetic,
But language I won't abuse.

1971 Ford Mustang

While I was a freshman in college,
My father traded in one Mustang for another,
In 1974.

I came home for Thanksgiving,
And there you were,
Canary Yellow and beige inside.
My love for you I could not hide.

I told my parents I was going to a high school basketball game,
Then I changed my mind.
I went to a store and bought some magazines.
Then I saw some high school friends.
That night I learned to play pretend.
As I pulled out of the parking space,

A fender bender, I hurt your face.
A tiny piece of you was left behind.
Just a little bit of your front corner.
I shook my head, I thought it was a dream.
I was afraid, but I had a scheme.
I acted like nothing was wrong.
My secret was safe,
Until this song.

1985 Chevy Camaro

You were my first brand new car.
I bought you in 1985.
A coworker was jealous,
But, hey, I was just some guy with a new Camaro.
I drove you to relatives to show you off.

Black, my favorite color at the time,
Inside and out.
And when I got you,
I felt like a shout.

I thought I was cool
In my huge, geeky glasses.
I tried to meet women,
But they rejected my passes.
"By the way, did I tell you
I have a Camaro?"

On vacation I drove you to South Carolina.
I thought life was sweet,
That it couldn't be finer.

About a year later,
I stopped next to a hater
At a red light.
He looked at me and my car.
Then he saw my glasses,
And said, "What a waste of a car."
I felt like driving to the nearest bar,
But I drove to the eye doctor instead.
He took the glasses off my head.
I wore contact lenses for ten years.

In 1989 I said, "Goodbye, old friend."
You shiny black car,
I loved you till the end.
I drove you in good times,
As well as the bad.
You knew when I was happy.
You knew when I was sad.

Snow

The snow falls swiftly.
Nature shows us the true way
To survive anger.

1990 Mazda Miata

It was love at first sight,
At the New York Auto Show,
In April of eighty-nine,
When I saw your sign.

It said prototype.
I believed all I heard,
For it wasn't just hype.

On the way home, I stopped at the dealer.
I had every intention of sending out feelers.
They answered my questions,
And I felt great.
$16,000,
A price I couldn't hate.
They put me on a list,
Number nine at the dealer.
I had to wait nine months,
But I was a big wheeler.

I told people at work,
I told friends and relations,
About my new car.
Waiting tested my patience.
I waited and waited,
For months and months.
Read stories, saw photos,
Much more than once.

I first saw you on the road in July,
And I felt like such a lucky guy.
I thought it was true,
What people did say,
That every dog has its day.

As I'm writing this poem,
I'm taking a break,
But the feeling of joy,
I just couldn't shake.

I finally met you,
In the August heat.
In Mariner Blue,
You looked so sweet.

I was living without fear,
Because you were named
Car of The Year.
You became part of the culture.
Comics joked about you on TV.
And finally, finally I felt free.
While buyers paid extra to have you,
They paid premiums like vultures.
I had to pay $800 myself,
But you really helped my mental health.

Convertible you,
With the wind in my hair,
I drove you each day,
To work with such care.
Admiring looks and passionate glances,
Who would think that I had the chances.
Compliments here, and compliments there.
Compliments, compliments everywhere.

Bug eyes popped up from your hood.
I was the envy of the neighborhood.
The grill you had was an oval grin.
I couldn't hide the joy within.

I went through two new convertible tops,
And a new transmission.
I even got a new engine.

We lived through thirteen years,
Over 120,000 miles.
But there had to be an end to the smiles.
I was having a rough time at my job.
I was a nice guy, I was no snob,
But it wasn't funny.
I didn't have much money.
I was having trouble making ends meet,
When in 2002 we had to part.
I sat for the last time in your seat.
It almost broke my heart.

Wedding Vow

As we gather in this place,
I see my future in your face.
I promise,
That every second,
Of every minute,
Of every hour,
Of every day,
I will be
The best man
I can be,
For you deserve no less.

1989 Buick LeSabre

My father bought you new for my mother,
As a 40th Wedding Anniversary present.
He drove you.

My mother drove you.
We all drove you.
Gray on the outside.
Gray within.
You were a sign of my father's love.
Little did we know
That three months later my father would be gone.

It was you, me and my mother,
Sharing an experience,
To which words cannot express.
We drove you in grief for several years.
We drove you in sadness,
We drove you in fears.

I liked you.
You were a nice car.
I thought I was turning into my father
Because I liked Buicks.
My mother and I drove you,
But not far.
Ten years later my mother passed.
I still drove you and paid for gas.

Then my uncle bought you,
With 32,000 miles on the odometer.

Honda 350

Like Martin Luther King I had a dream.
I saw a TV show about a man
With a motorcycle that traveled the country,
And changed people's lives.

Six years after that show was cancelled,
I had my chance.
I bought you, used.
I bought some camping gear.
I had no fear.

I was in my fourth semester,
At UConn in Storrs.
I was bored and depressed.
I went through such stress.
I felt like a rebel,
And sort of a loner.
I didn't use drugs, but some friends were stoners.
I rode you each day,
With the wind in my face.
I had my own ride.
I had my own space.

I rode you home from school.
A speed demon, I.
Eighty miles per hour
On the New Jersey Turnpike.
I thought it was cool,
But I was a fool.

I stayed home a few days.
I thought I was on my way,
But my parents were concerned.
You became a lemon.
I packed my backpack,
But my parents wanted me on the right track.
My mom said, "If you quit school now,
You'll never go back."
So I broke down and chickened out.

I stayed in town and transferred my school.
I tried to live by the Golden Rule.

I finished college, I got my degree.
I got married and had a family.
I was a consultant and that was great.
I've travelled to thirty states.
I guess you could say I've had some success,
But sometimes I wonder as I look back,
How my life would have panned out
If you weren't a lemon.

Corvette

Ever since I can recall,
You were my favorite car of all.
A car of style, a car of speed,
You are the only car I need.

You are on my bucket list.
I'll tell you now, I'll give you the gist.
I wanted you then, I want you now.
I'll work for you by the sweat on my brow.

One in green, or maybe gray,
I'll have you to drive some distant day.
Maybe I'll win the lottery.
So much to do, so much to see.

So many friends to aid with wealth,
I must maintain my mental health.
So down each distant road I'll go.
I'll own you someday. Yes, this I know.

Blood Red Vette

I've got a blood red Vette.
I'm gonna get you yet,
Driving down the highway.
We're gonna drink some wine, and feel so fine.
We're gonna do it my way.

Driving down the road of life,
Looking for a friend, a wife.
Someone with whom my life to share.
As we pass through life's ups and downs,
In cities, farms and suburban towns.
Someone who knows, someone who cares.
All that we've done, all that we know,
To share the work and fun and grow,
To be the best that we can be.
To cope with loss and share the gains,
To use each other and heal the pain,
To become a family.

My Birthday

(Born May 23, 1956 – Written May 23, 2016)
Today is my birthday, and I am 60.
I've seen lots of women, some are pretty.
I've had lots of ups and downs.
I've lived on farms, in cities and towns.
I've been happy. I've been sad.
I've done good things. I've been bad.

So in my life I've learned some things,
That I'd like to share this spring.
Everyone has lives that matter,
Even if you're mad as a hatter.
Everyone here has a purpose,
Even if it makes you nervous.

Do what you're good at. Do what you like,
Even if it's speaking behind a mike.
Don't let anyone steal your dream,
Or stand between you and your schemes.
Don't give up. Just be persistent.
On this matter I am insistent.
So these are the thoughts I think today.
Like Frank Sinatra, I did it my way.

I Am America

I live from sea to shining sea,
The land of the brave and home of the free.
On my flag pole, the Star Spangled Banner.
I teach my children how to have manners.
I am America the Beautiful,
The land of the dutiful.

I work hard and like to have fun.
I am battles lost and victories won.
I am Army and Navy, Marines and Air Force,
National Guard and Coast Guard, of course.
I'm tinker and tailor and soldier and spy,
I'll do what is right, look you in the eye.
I'm doctor and lawyer and nurse and clerk.
I am good people, and just a few jerks.

I am mother and father and daughter and son.
I give you the freedom to carry a gun.

People come here by plane, train and boat.
I freed the slaves and gave women the vote.
I'm the greatest nation in the history of earth,
I'm the place where freedom gave birth.
The wealthiest nation in history,

And why? It is no mystery.
The land of opportunity.

I'm white and black and yellow and red,
I'm Joe the Plumber and famous dead.
I am the world's most powerful nation,
Despite some poverty and inflation.
I am Christian and Muslim and Jew,
There's even room for atheists, too.
I'm capitalism and free enterprise.
My freedom of speech uncovers the lies.

I'm city and suburb and rural farm.
I try to keep my people from harm.
I'm skyscrapers, schools, churches and banks.
On Thanksgiving we all give thanks.

I'm Yankees and Giants and Knicks and Mets.
The Dallas Cowboys and even the Jets,
I'm the Chicago Bulls and Chicago Bears.
I am a nation that loves and cares.
I am a country that's better than China.
I'm also the San Fran Forty Niners.

I'm Taquan, Mohammed, Rajeesh and Fred.
Freedom of thought is in my head.

I'm Republican, Democrat, Libertarian.
There's even a place for Rastafarians.
Bald eagle and the buffalo,
I encourage people to learn and grow.

Washington, Lincoln, Kennedy, Reagan,
My short history has only begun.
I'm Hillary Clinton and Donald Trump,
Citizen Kane and Forrest Gump.

To my enemies I'll shout,
"You can knock me down,
But you can't knock me out."
I am America.

Cardinal

Oh, beauteous red bird,
Friendly flying up and down,
A gift from life itself,
Saying hello in the parking lot.
Appearing weeks later,
I knew it was you again.

My sweet, fine feathered friend,
Saying hello and lifting my mood.

Good Advice

Take your meds as indicated.
Don't ever do them when you get frustrated.
Go to program as much as you can.
Don't worry too much, life has a plan.
Watch out for sugar and foods high in salt.
Just lock this all up in your mental vault.

A healthy heart and a healthy brain
Go hand in hand, and help life to remain.
Depression and stress cause heart disease,
So use coping skills, please, please, please.
Cut down on smoking. Quit if you can.
Vaping is another plan.
Use a patch or medication,
Hypnotism or meditation.
Quitting helps your taste and smell.
It makes you healthy, feeling well.

Make sure you get eight hours of sleep.
Get some rest, your soul to keep.
Cut down on soda, coffee and tea.
I hope you don't think I'm too bossy.
If you want to stay alive,
See your doctor every year after age 35.
Stay away from the street drugs and booze.
They can leave you even more confused.
I know that you're avoiding the feelings that you feel,
But you've got to work them out in order to heal.

Red Nose Day

There's a special day in the month of May,
When people look like clowns as they go upon their way,
When the poor and the children have their say.
But to change the world it takes more than just a day.

So give what you will and give what you can.
So just be responsible and take part in life's plan,
Because it's hard eating from a garbage can.
Go to Walgreens, watch NBC and be a fan.

Do it for the kids and do it for the poor.
Wear a red nose when you walk out the door.
Otherwise, what are you living for?
Put on your red nose, feel strong and sure.

Sean Penn

I like the actor named Sean Penn.
I'll see his movies, again and again.

Looking In Your Eyes

From the beginning of space and time,
Through the creation of prose and rhyme,
It's something that I'll never forget,
The instant that we met.
Looking in your eyes.

The green of grass and the blue of sky.
Oh, I feel like such a lucky guy,
Because I see it all in your eyes.
You are such a special friend.
You do not play pretend,
As I'm looking in your eyes.

Looking in your eyes,
I can not disguise
The way I feel for you.
A love so great and true.
Looking in your eyes.
Your mind, your heart, your soul.
Sharing time with you is my goal.
Looking in your eyes.
Looking in your eyes.

I see sunsets of one thousand suns,
And the trials that you've overcome.
The laughter, sadness, joy and tears,
The life you've lived throughout the years,
Looking in your eyes.

As I feed off of your energy,
Something's happening between you and me.
Do your eyes see as you look at me?
I must say this, I will not lie.
I'll recall you until I die,
And looking in your eyes.

Looking in your eyes,
I can not disguise
The way I feel for you.
A love so great and true.

Looking in your eyes.
Your mind, your heart, your soul.

Sharing time with you is my goal.
Looking in your eyes.
Looking in your eyes.

For K

I'm glad you came over last Friday night.
What you said just made things more right.
I know of your struggles,
I know of your fights.
I want you to know you bring me delight.

I don't want to scare, make you anxious or nervous.
I just want you to know that you have a purpose.
I don't write this to judge you or criticize,
But I care about you and I'll tell you no lies.

You speak of saying things you can't take back,
But in your heart there's nothing you lack.
We've all said things that we regret,
And I know very well that it's hard to forget.
You shouldn't be so hard on yourself.
I'm just concerned about your health.

I know you're concerned about your life.
It can be frustrating, full of strife.
I know how it feels. I've felt it before,
Like you want to give up, and walk out the door.
I know sometimes people are judgmental and mean,
But I think you should be treated like a queen.

I think you're too busy, though you like to work.
I hope you don't think that I'm a jerk.
You might want to cut back on the hours a bit,
Find a less stressful job that's a better fit.

It all builds up and causes you stress,
When you try to do more and end up with less.
Those people that say that you've screwed up your life?
Enough already! Enough with the strife!
Get away from them now. Just walk out the door,
Or yes them to death, like I've done before.
Don't let these people harsh your mellow.
Just go outside and see the sun, yellow.

You might be tempted to return to old ways,
To have wild nights to cope with the days.
I know how it feels, I understand,
But you deserve a better man.
Not someone that shares just a few hours,
For you are a fragile, delicate flower.

I think you might need a man who stays,
Not just for hours, but weeks, months and days.
Someone who will help you turn the tide,
Because life can be a wild ride.
Someone who will be there and care and listen,
When the tears start to fall on your face and glisten.
Someone to work with and learn and grow,
As time passes by, a soulmate to know.

I want you to know, whatever you choose,
Whether you win or whether you lose,
Through the times happy or through the times sad,
Through the good times and through the bad.
I want you to know that there's nothing I lack.

No matter what, I've got your back.
I am your friend, trustworthy and loyal.
You deserve to be treated like a family royal.

You can come over at any time,
To watch movies, talk or read my rhymes.
You can come over, day or night,
Because I think you're out of sight.
I'll listen to you as I look in your eyes,
Without any judgement or criticize.
I'll tell you the truth and give you advice.
You can take it or leave it or slap my face.
I will not lie or play pretend,
I'll be your friend until life ends.

I know what you want. I know how you feel.
What went wrong, and what's the deal?
Why did I do that? Why did I do this?
I want a house, a family and kids.
I want my son back to see what he did.
I just want you to know that you still have time,
I guess that's the point of this long rhyme.
I'm hoping this poem gives you wings.
I know just how you feel,
Because I want the same things.

Focus on the positive and seek solutions,
To deal with society and make contributions.
Focus on what can be done,
To ensure your battle is won.
Focus on what you can control,
Not what you can't – you'll lose your soul.

Avoid complainers and energy drainers.
Negative people and all disdainers.

Hang out with those on the bright side of life,
To help you avoid and overcome strife.
Smile and laugh. Be warm, open and caring.
I'm already impressed with your generous sharing.

Break the shackles of worry and stress.
To those you trust you can confess.
Live your life, happy and free,
Share time with positive people like me.
Assert a position and set boundaries,
But don't make needless enemies.
Guard your time and commitments,
Know when to say no.
Think and stay calm
When anger grows.

Accomplishment, meaning in life,
Relationships and positive emotion.
The secret to inner happiness is in that magic potion.
Our habits shape our future and even our existence.
It's important to be disciplined and have persistence.
If we change our habits, we can change our lives,
So this is how we do it, this is why we strive.

I'll tell you one thing you can do because I'm an honest guy.
One thing that's important is to simply simplify.
Turn off your phone and email and life's other distractions,
So you can spend more time with those you love,
And have mutual attraction.

You need free time to appreciate and enjoy,
Especially time with your little boy.
Be aware of your feelings and thinking,
Especially when you feel bad and stink thinking.

You are not always what you think and feel,
So know the difference between the false and the real.

Being mindful every day
Can help you as you travel upon your way.
Be spacious, accepting and show compassion.
It will help your life and fashion.

Have some joy at home each day,
Before you go along the way.
Find happiness in little things,
Not fancy cars or diamond rings.
If your mind is healthy, you will flourish.
An optimal state of being you'll cherish.

Take some time for quiet reflection.
Don't worry about all the rejection.
Rise above your thought's whirlpool,
And look within. You won't be fooled.
What do you aspire to?
In your past, you surely knew.
The burdens seem to disappear.
When you have perspective, you lose the fear.

You've got to flip the switch today.
Focus on good, sweep the bad away.
Be grateful and positive.
That's the way that you should live.
How do you feel? What do you think?
Love, peace and calm take you from the brink.
You'll be successful at everything.

Let the forces of life move you and soothe you.
Have an attitude of gratitude.

Be open to the possibility,
And life will bring opportunity.

Don't make things personal.
Don't let it become internal.
Nothing others say or do
Is ever about you.
It's about them, my trusted friend.
It's mind games and playing pretend.
They have issues, and it's up to them.

Forget about limits you place on yourself,
They're not real. They're illusions of your mental health.
Though you've got to examine
The worst that can happen,
You should know that it probably won't.
So if you feel fearful, or even tearful, don't.

Practice loving kindness and loving-kindness,
For everyone you meet.
It brings good vibes while you're alive,
Even for strangers on the street.

Be aware of your energy,
And the energy around you.
Some people bring joy,
Some people destroy,
Some people will astound you.

Email and news and music and books
Can take you away from the calm,

But wonder and joy never destroy,
And act like a healing balm.

You've asked me how to find your purpose.
I'll tell you now, life can be a circus.
First you need to find your center,
Whether you're an owner or a renter.
This poem has beaucoup advice,
I give it because I think you're nice.
I hope you conquer all your fears.
I hope you'll find some answers here,
But most lie in your heart and mind,
In quiet moments you shall find.

Think of future, present and past,
Of what you choose to end and last,
Of things you've done and want to do,
Of what is false and what is true,
Of who you liked and who you hated,
Events you mourned and celebrated.
Think about the whats and whys,
Of why you've laughed and why you cried.
Think of things done well and poorly.
You will find the answers, surely.

You'll find your center, purpose and future,
If your self you'll love and nurture.
All these truths will come to you,
And you will know just what to do.

When in your home you're sad and lonely,
Just stop by or you can call me.
We can watch TV or movies,
I will help you feel so groovy.
We can hike in fields of clover,
Until your problems are done and over.
Or we can just sit down and chat,
Until you've got the answers down pat.

I will provide a listening ear,
And you will conquer all your fears.
You'll reach that milestone you savor,
Regaining life's wonderful flavor.
Now that you've read this, the seeds are sown.
You're one of the greatest people I've ever known.

Frenemies

You're not really a friend,
Though I've known you since first grade.
I won't play pretend.
You've affected choices I've made.
Crazy thoughts and actions, too.
Depression, anxiety – I've named you.
Trying to get out of bed,
With shaky nerves and thoughts in my head.
Diagnosed in 95,
I wondered why I was alive.
It's been a struggle ever since then.
You are my enemy, not my friend.

Frenemies.
Not really friends, but enemies.
Oh, anxiety,
You've been too close to me.
And you, depression,
With that feeling of rejection.
Go away. Go far, far away.

It's been a real struggle.
Self harm and anger running wild.

No one to cuddle.
Pain from the trauma of a child.

An outcast, a hated man.
No hope. No love, just a suicide plan.

Can't work. Can't walk down the street.
In these surroundings I can't compete.

But wait, there's hope in my life.
Meds and programs, but still no wife.
I appreciate the smaller things,
Like love, friendship and birds with wings.

Frenemies.
Not really friends, but enemies.
Oh, anxiety.
You've been too close to me.
And you, depression,
With that feeling of rejection.
Go away. Go far, far away.

American Might

American might
Brings powerful strength
Against the evil.

Red Shoes

They called to me at the mall in Cherry Hill.
I could have resisted, but I didn't have the will.
Without hesitation, I bought them on the spot.
Now I wear them every day, so proud of what I've got.

Yes, I wear them daily. I wear them on my feet.
People say they like them and it makes me feel so neat.
I'm living in the moment. No, I'm not confused.
I wear my red shoes because they help me beat the blues.

Elvis and the angels are gonna have to wait,
'Cause I'm wearing them tonight.
I'm running late for a date.
Red shoes, red shoes.

Sometimes they're the red in my red, white and blue.
I wear them to the program and sometimes to the zoo.
Sometimes people say that I've got nothing to gain,
But my red shoes help me get through the trauma and the pain.

I walk in them now, but not fast as I can,
Because I'm getting older now and I have a master plan.
I walk and I talk and I stop to smell the roses.
My life is getting better and everybody knows this.
Red shoes, red shoes, red shoes, red shoes.
Elvis and the angels are gonna have to wait,
'Cause I'm wearing them tonight.
I'm running late for a date.
Red shoes, red shoes.

Red shoes, red shoes, red shoes, red shoes.
Elvis and the angels are gonna have to wait,
'Cause I'm wearing them tonight.
I'm running late for a date.
Red shoes, red shoes.

Scatology

This word is about doo doo and poop,
Like you find in a chicken coop.
You wouldn't want it on your stoop.
Sometimes they also call it crap.
You wouldn't want it on your lap.

This word is about urine and piss,
So what do you make of this?
It's also called taking a whiz.
Sometimes they also call it pee.
It all comes out of you and me.

Derek Jeter

I've been a Yankees fan my entire life,
Whether I was single or married to a wife.
I've been truly loyal through the thick and the thin.
They've had some losing seasons but they know just how to win.

They're the greatest team in the annals of sports,
Whether you watch them in a suit or a tee shirt and shorts.
They've won the most awards, pennants and World Series.

How can you root for other teams?
Don't you get so weary?

There have been many legends on this team of might and fame,
Some of the greatest men to ever play the game,
But nothing can be finer, no, nothing can be sweeter
Than a hit off the bat of mister Derek Jeter.

The Iron Man, the Yankee Clipper and of course, the Babe.
The runners ran, the hitters hit, pitchers got wins and saves.
The Scooter, "Holy cow" and Oklahoma Mick,
In the 1970's Gene Michael was "The Stick."
Yogi Berra was a funny guy, it's true.
He hit his share of home runs into the sky of blue.
I even know about a Yank whose name was Elston Howard.
After all their games the Yankees headed for the shower.
In '61 Roger Maris broke Babe's home run record.
Baseball gave him an asterisk. I'm sure he felt rejected.
And then there are the pitchers, like Ford and Lyle and Wells,
Who gave opposing batters a little taste of hell.
Mike Kekich and Fritz Peterson were really, really tight.
It was a big time scandal when they traded wives at night.
Then there's Bobby Mercer and Reggie Jackson.
When he came to town he was a big attraction.
They called him by his nickname which was Mister October.
Let's not forget Thurman Munson. Too bad his life is over.

There have been may legends on this team of might and fame,
Some of the greatest men to ever play the game,
But nothing can be finer, no, nothing can be sweeter
Than a hit off the bat of mister Derek Jeter.

Now he is retired, a Yank his whole career.
He still has many fans who love him, from afar and near.

He's an author now, and he tells of his exploits.
He is still respected in Boston and Detroit.

There have been many legends on this team of might and fame,
Some of the greatest men to ever play the game,
But nothing can be finer, no, nothing can be sweeter
Than a hit off the bat of mister Derek Jeter.

Chipmunk

Hello, little chipmunks,
Climbing up a tree,
For me to see,
Two days in a row.
So, what do you know?

You and my bird friends
Stop by to say hello,
Providing some sunshine,
As I learn and grow.
I hope it never ends.

I liked Alvin and you,
When I was a kid.
Sometimes I played pretend,
With some things I did.
I admit that it's true.

Christian Brothers are a lot like monks.
They like to make wine, but they don't get drunk.
I like your TV show about Monk the detective.

I hope no one thinks that I'm defective.
Now I've played this word association game.
I hope no one thinks that I'm insane.

Everything But The Oink

When you think about your food,
Notice how it affects your mood.

I've had ham and I've had spam.
I've got to admit I'm a pretty big fan.

When I go to shop and I see a pork chop,
It makes me so happy I want to hop.

I tried pigs feet once and I wasn't "a-feared,"
I said it was good but I felt kind of weird.

What is that smell I smell you makin'?
Why, it's breakfast, of course, of eggs and bacon!
Bacon is the candy of meats.
I don't have it often, but oh, what a treat!

I've never had a pig or pork snout.
I don't really care what it's about.

Every once in a while, I'll have some baloney.
I like to eat it with macaroni.
Now, I've had beef and I've had chicken,
But barbequed pork is finger lickin'.
So as you sit and view food on your plate,
Just meditate or contemplate,
About our porcine animal friends

Who don't put on airs or play pretend.
And then it will hit you! BANG!
KADOINK!
Then you'll want to say or sing,
"When it comes to pigs we use everything –
Everything but the oink."

New Clothes

I do it every once in a while.
It makes me feel better and helps me to smile.
I do it once every three or four years,
And it helps me to push back the tears.

Sometimes it's like livin' in a dream.
It helps me improve my self esteem.
Just as long as I get the same inseam,
Shopping at the store with the wood beams.

So do not judge me and do not hate,
Or think you are in control of my fate,
As you watch me shop like a fashion plate,
Wherever I go to buy new clothes.

You Bring The Thunder
(For Beyonce)

You bring the thunder,
And you sing in the rain.
There's a sense of wonder,
As you share joy and pain,
And when the winds outside rage,
You ignore the weather and sing on stage.

You learned to dance and you started to sing,
For fame and fortune and everything.
You sang in a salon and you sang in church.
You were in Girl's Tyme with songs that rhyme.
You were on TV for all to see,
On a show we all know,
Called Star Search.
You were in Something Fresh and a group called Cliché'.
You were in the Dolls. It was your "Destinay."
Then you made it with Destiny's Child,
When you sang and danced as fans went wild.

You bring the thunder,
And you sing in the rain.
There's a sense of wonder,
As you share joy and pain,
And when the winds outside rage,
You ignore the weather and sing on stage.

You weren't Killing Time on Men In Black.
Why Do Fools Fall In Love?
You were on the sound track.

I can see why you'd Get On The Bus.
I understand why fans make a fuss.
You can sing, dance, act and shout –
I knew you would Work It Out.
You're a Soul Survivor and a real big striver.
You were in an Austin Powers movie,
And you made Austin Powers feel groovy.
You've been Dangerously, Crazy, Drunk In Love.
Compared to other singers, you rank far above.
Your birthday falls on September 4th.
Your fame spreads east, south, west and north.
You were in Dreamgirls and won an award.
I follow your career and I don't get bored.
You sang "Honesty", Billy's song in Japan.
I knew all along you had a plan.
At times you are known as Sasha Fierce.
I wonder if your ears are pierced.
You made Jay Z Put A Ring On It.
When he made a CD, you would sing on it.
You live in a House of Dereon.
Do you know anyone named Leon?
You did a song called "Video Phone."
You sang in groups, duos and all alone.
You spoke to a Lady on the Telephone.
The woman in you was with Jessica S.
You couldn't do more and you couldn't do less.
You sing your hits and you Do It Again.
You're so real. You don't play pretend.
You were there on nine eleven.
Your voice is a little taste of heaven.
To me, you smell like the Rush of Heat.
You sing and dance to an R and B beat.
You're Irreplaceable, this you should know –
Listen, Hollywood, you're still on the grow.
When you drive, do you go on Green Light?

You sing all day and you sing at night.
Your fans love you, Flaws and All.
How is Miss Gaga?
Does she still call?

You bring the thunder,
And you sing in the rain.
There's a sense of wonder,
As you share joy and pain,
And when the winds outside rage,
You ignore the weather and sing on stage.

There's one more opinion I'd like to share –
The hell with Becky with the good hair.

Unforgiving

We're born to die,
It is no lie.
We start going downhill
At twenty five.

The seconds, the minutes, the hours, the days,
We all get set in our own little ways.
The weeks, the months, the seasons and years,
Through good times and bad,
Happy and sad,
Giggles and tears.

It's a hard world to make a living,
For age is our battle,
And it's unforgiving.

Bucket List

As you go through life,
And you wonder, "What's this?"
Through your joy and strife,
It's a bucket list.

The things you do before you pass,
Some dreams die and some dreams last.
And if you accomplish your life long goals,
Consider yourself a fortunate soul.

I would like to fly in space,
With dignity, comfort, speed and grace.
I'll eat at the Bellagio in LV,
Before I touch eternity.

Some day I'd like to own a Corvette.
The day I get one, I won't forget.
So much I'd like to see and do,
As I grow every day and learn things new.

Fame

Andy Warhol said it best.
Fifteen minutes of fame,
Then it's back to the rest.

Big Business Versus The Common Man

He worked for the company for forty years.
He thought he was set on a path free of tears,
But they lied to him and his family is sad.
Now he's dead 'cause he felt really bad.

The day before he got his pension,
The boss came along and forgot to mention,
"You're fired today. No job, no pension.
No money for you, so take a hike."

He went home in his car, and the very next day,
He had a heart attack and passed away.
No more watching his grandchildren at play.
He died in the ER in Galloway.

It's big business versus the common man.
It's all part of the money plan.
They work you for hours and pay a few cents.
To me, it doesn't make any sense.
It's just a source of pain and stress.

You can be trustworthy, loyal and kind,
But they will work you and work you right out of your mind.
They don't care how you plan your career,
It's all about the money, my dear.

You work and you toil for days and days,
But after a year you get no raise.
Now if frustration you display,
They send you out on your merry way.

Now if you think I seem too jaded,
It's true that all my hopes have faded,
So in this song I've serenaded.
Through fire we've been consecrated.

It's big business versus the common man.
It's all part of the money plan.
They work you for hours and pay a few cents.
To me, it just doesn't make any sense.
It's just a source of pain and stress.

LGBT

I don't have a problem with L, G or B,
But, for the life of me, I can't fathom T.
Maybe it's me.
What's a single guy to do?
It isn't getting better yet.
They're taking over the alphabet.

Jimmy

They called him Jimmy. Yes, Jimmy H.
His father had a problem with rage.
Jimmy had problems with his neck and hip,
And when you gave him trouble he would give you some lip.
No, no, no. He wouldn't back down.
He lived in Arkansas and Oklahoma,
But he was raised in Jersey towns.

He had it rough,
But he's real tough.
He wrote songs, sang and played guitar.
Many people think he's gonna go far.
Jimmy. Jimmy H.

He was always outspoken and brash.
He didn't bother with people's trash.
Although he's been homeless, addicted and poor,
He doesn't use drugs or drink anymore.
He's seen the error of his ways.
Now he sings at night and writes songs during the days.

He had it rough,
But he's real tough.
He wrote songs, sang and played guitar.
Many people think he's gonna go far.
Jimmy. Jimmy H.

Losing Battle

Time goes on,
An ebb and flow.
What have we accomplished?
What do we know?

Generations, future and past,
Nothing ever really lasts.
The sands of time
Wear thin on the skin.
We all lose it all.
We never win.

We're marching towards death,
Like a herd of cattle.
We're fighting the fight,
But it's a losing battle.

Cards

One night I had a dream,
That I was playing poker,
And I had three queens.
A guy had two jacks,
And thought he had won.
I knew it was war,
And we had just begun.
He reached for the chips,
With a confident stare.
I said, "Hold it, man!
Just hold it right there!
I don't mean to be obscene,
But I've won this round.
I've got three queens!"
So he gave me the chips.
He gave them right back.
I was happy –
I won the whole rack.

Little Pink House

(For Muhammed Ali)

He was born a black man in a little pink house,
In 1942 in the heart of the South.
No one had ever seen a man like him,
So fast and strong,
So pretty,
So full of vigor and vim.

He floated like a butterfly,
And stung like a bee.
He was an honest man
Who went down in history.

As the Louisville Lip, he never sold out.
In the ring he would prance and shout.
He showed resilience,
Which is what life's about.
He thrilled the millions
With his boxing knockouts.

He beat "The Bear" and "The Gorilla," too
In the Thrilla in Manilla,
He won fair and square.
With the "Rope-A-Dope," George Foreman got screwed.
He beat Spinks and Norton, too.

He jumped through each hoop,
And he passed every test.
He was true to himself.

That's why he was best.
Now he's "got plenty of time to rest."

He fought many battles, in and out of the ring.
He was boxing's number one king.
The government was his most difficult fight.
The second toughest was his first wife.
Every time he lost, he would come back stronger,
Until he couldn't fight any longer.

He taught us some lessons we all should learn,
While he fought and made all the money he earned,
Like never judge a person by their faith or their race,
And be honest to all right up to their face.
He'd defeat opponents and make predictions.
He stood up for his own convictions.
He was a man who spoke in rhymes.
He was a man carved from his times.
In twenty one years he had sixty one fights,
He had more than his share of pain and delight.
To ignore him was impossible,
As he tried to be responsible.
You loved him or you hated him.
You praised him or berated him.
He spoke for those who had no voice.
He chose for those who had no choice.
He was a villain and a hero.
He was unwillin' to be a zero.

He won the championship three different times,
With fortitude, skill and an iron spine.
His record was fifty-six and five,
And he made a difference while he was alive.
He was willing to back up his words with facts,
And the way you saw him was no act.

He was a man ahead of his time.
He evaded the draft, but he paid for his crime.
He lost over three years of his boxing prime.

He lived in a house in Cherry Hill.
To watch him box was a real thrill.
His final battle was Parkinson's,
And he lost a few fights but mostly, he won.
Ali was smart. He knew where to stand,
And mostly he fought with his chin, feet and hands.
What made him special was his will,
And he backed that up with his boxing skill.
He stood up for his rights with nothing to gain,
And you must give him credit for handling pain.
He went against society's grain.

The Self

We're all an onion that's peeled away,
As we pass through time to the present day.
What more is there to say?
Some people doubt and some people pray.

Who are you and who is me?
We're searching for the truth to see.
To find that atom of the truth,
To live forever, to save our youth.

In your life you may never know.
Sometimes it goes fast, sometimes it goes slow.
You take two steps back but you think you grow.

I've got to live, my point to prove.
Do I stand my ground or do I move?
Who am I and who are you?
I seek for what is real and true.
We all seek our identity,
To live to the fullest,
And finally break free.
It's the story of humanity,
The self in you and the self in me.

Do you need to be loved,
Or do you love to be needed?
Take this advise as I have heeded.

Identity

Identity.
What is it to you?
What is it to me?

Biological.
Anthropological.
Political.
Social.
Racial.

Identity.
What is it to you?
What is it to me?

The self is ambiguous.
What is it to you?
What is it to me?

We seek our own identity.
What is it to you?
What is it to me?

In finding ourselves,
We lose others,
Like mothers and fathers,
Sisters and brothers.

Identity.
What is it to you?
What is it to me?

Internal conflicts in place and time,
Like prose in poetry,
Or prose that rhymes.

It's a struggle that ends not.
Who am I?
I just forgot.

Identity.
What is it to you?
What is it to me?

Before you come and take my hand,
Do you even understand?

Identity.
What is it to you?
What is it to me?

Eternal worlds overlap in the self,
And it affects my mental health.

Identity.
What is it to you?
What is it to me?

Oaks

I used to come here, to a place called Oaks.
You get better here. It is no joke.
It's a place to help you cope,
When you're down in the dumps,
At the end of your rope.
You can go outside and have a smoke.
I know a couple of guys named Dave.
In financial management, you learn how to save.
I talk news and politics with Katie,
We both like to know what's been going on lately.
Then there is my good friend, Kevin.
This place is a little taste of heaven.
Another guy I know is Sean.
It seems so different when he's gone.
I also know a guy named Kareem.
I want to help his automotive dream.

There's Liz, Alexia and Breuana,
I wonder if they like Rihanna.
Have they ever heard of the group, Santana?
Have they been out west, out to Montana?
There's Lauren and Rachel and, of course, Erin.
When you speak, they thank you for sharin'.

The rhyming pair is Maria and Sophia.
They both make all our issues look clearer.
There's Chris and Jim and don't forget Ed,

They help me feel calm when I lay down my head.
Of course, my goal group leader, Alice,
Makes me feel like a king in a palace.
Don't forget Miss Joy, Prudence and Courtney.
So many people here support me.
The nurses, the doctors, the rest of the staff,
They all take my tears and turn them to laughs.

My best friend, Susan, I met her here.
I'm conquering my loneliness fear.
I came here, anxious and alone,
And met some of the greatest people I've ever known.
I listened to all and I followed the plan,
And now I'm a better human and man.

The Media

When you watch the TV news,
It often tends to bring the blues.
When you read the news in papers,
They don't tell you all the capers.
When you hear the news on the radio,
Before you opine, just take it slow.

Don't get caught up in sensations,
That hide what happens in our nation.
To find the truth,
Just teach your youth,
To take many college courses,
And get the news from many sources.
To find the truth, it is not scary.
Just be cautious, sly and wary.
Watch the news that's balanced and fair,

And tell your friends to share, share, share.
Don't go by instincts just like an animal,
Just tune in daily to Fox News Channel.

The Dream

I had a dream while I was dead,
That I was still alive,
Livin' night to night and day to day,
Doin' what it took to survive.

The dreams I had died long ago,
In the days of my youth.
I wonder if it was worth the price,
In my lifelong pursuit of the truth.

So many people lose their dreams,
Getting lost in the fog.
You work and you work and then you sleep,
Like some meaningless, empty cog.

Reach you goal and you're fortunate,
A fortunate daughter or son.
Then you can rest and breathe easily,
As you wait for your life to be done.

Where Did The Music Go?

I remember the music playing,
In the days of my youth.
There was nothing like it to this day,
Though some thought it was uncouth.

The early foundations of rock and roll,
Sixties pop and Motown soul.
Elvis the King did everything.
The music was out of control.

The Beatles made you scream and shout,
As old folks tried to figure it out.
The Monkees believed,
We were not deceived,
As old folks continued to pout.

Dylan spoke for all of us,
As we rode on the Freedom Bus.
Old folks looked on in disgust,
As young people wondered who to trust.

When I see and hear the music today,
There's something that I have to say.
It was so good back in the day.
There's one thing that I want to know.
Where did the music go?

I Don't Want To Fall

I don't want to fall for you.
I don't want to like you too much.
I don't want to look in your eyes.
I don't want to feel your touch.

I don't want to be too nice,
But I don't want to be cold as ice.
I don't want to look at you twice.
I don't want to taste your spice.

I don't want to be surprised.
I don't want to tell any lies.
I don't want to fantasize.
I don't want to shed tears or cry.

I don't want to feel the pain.
I don't want to walk in the rain.

I want to walk in sunshine.
I want my life to be fine.

I don't want my heart to be broken,
But I don't want words left unspoken.
My memories are a token,
Of how I feel for you.

Like My Father

I never thought it would happen,
I thought as I sat down, crappin'.
Here I am at the age of sixty,
The head of my own family.

I'm turning into my father,
But it does not really bother.
I'm not just a zero,
But he was a hero.
I'm trying to do what I ought to.

I'm starting to like the Buicks.
But buy one? I don't think I'd do it.
I long for the days,
When rock was the craze,
Like my father longed for swing music.

Heart of Gold
(Made Of Steel)

They all said he was a strange little man,
Who tried to live his life according to plan,
But poop happens and the crap hits the fan,
So what's a man to do?

He had a heart of gold,
But he was made of steel.
He hated to be told,
What to do and what to feel.

He lived in a world
Part fantasy, part real.

Some folks thought he was led by the spirit.
Sometimes he'd hoard and sometimes he'd share it.
He had a pig's nose and the teeth of a ferret.
He was a hated man.

He wasn't afraid to share his views.
He liked to keep up with politics and news.
They pulled the rug out from under him,
And put him to the screws,
But he lived as best he can.
He wasn't perfect but he was a man.
One day he came to an untimely end,
'Cause he wouldn't play the game or play pretend.
He wasn't like the rest of us.
He tried to be their friend.
No one seemed to care.

He had a heart of gold,
But he was made of steel.
He hated to be told
What to do and what to feel.
He lived in a world
Part fantasy, part real.

He had a heart of gold,
But he was made of steel.
A heart of gold,
But made of steel.
Heart of gold,
Made of steel.
Oh, heart of gold…

For Those Of Faith

Sometimes I write poetry right away.
Sometimes I let it simmer for a day,

To gather my thoughts and do research,
For in a way, my mind is my church.

You can believe what you want to believe.
Just mind your own business,
But don't be deceived.
You've got the right to believe what you want,
But it doesn't give you rights to bully or taunt.

As I live my life in my own way,
From night to night and day to day,
Don't go away.
Please stay.
I want to be hear
Your encouraging words.

Life

What really matters is death and birth,
And your time on planet earth.
Nothing is permanent. Nothing lasts.
In an instant, the future becomes the past.
Too often we lose opportunities,
The greatness in you and the greatness in me.
So when upon these things you ponder,
Do not live your life to squander.

Fantasy

I've got this fantasy in my brain,
So my heart won't break or feel the pain.
I can think at every opportunity.
It doesn't cost me anything.
It's totally free.
Why pay the money to take a girl out?
If you're poor, you know what I'm talkin' about.

When things don't work out the way that you plan,
And you live your life the best that you can,
There's one way to reconcile life in your mind.
I call it my own fantasy,
At least that's what I find.
I live in my mind what you live for real,
So don't tell me what to think, do or feel.

I Don't Care

In a certain time and place,
I came across you, and saw your face.
We've got things in common, you and I,
Like our love of nature and the sky.

I don't care that you have issues,
Though I feel for you.
I'll go out and buy you tissues.
Believe it because it's true.

I don't care that you smoke.
I know you do it to help you cope.

I don't care that sometimes you drink,
I don't care what anyone thinks.
You can sip anytime from my coffee mug.
I don't care just how you look.
One look in your eyes and that's all it took.

I'll tell you what, I'd like to share.
I'll tell you exactly why I care.
I care about your quick wit,
For it's not often that I run across it.
I care about your intelligence,
About things that are relevant.
I care about your generosity,
And how you share with others and me.
I care about your curiosity,
About all things, like land and sea.
As you can see, my heart doesn't judge,
And I try not to hold a grudge.
I see you as you can be,

And that's okay with me.

Contradictions

Who is the patriot in you and me?
The one that changes reality.
We are a nation of contradictions,
That's why it's so hard to make predictions.

The man who wrote "all men are... equal"
Is grist for a movie and a sequel,
For he owned slaves in days of old,
So to make such acclaim was really bold.

It's a contradiction, but we all live it out,
Though some don't know what they're talking about.
Our founding fathers saw ideals,
And tried to change old ways that were real.

So who is to say what's right and what's wrong?
If you have an opinion, then write a song.
We're what we are. What? We are who we are.
Though some are not able, all reach for the stars.

So if it's true freedom that you seek,
Come to America. We are unique.
I fight for this country, where I was born,
Though some think the government's outdated and worn.
We live in turbulent days and ages,
Where fire burns and anger rages.
ML King and the Kennedys
Tried making life better for you and me.
They were shot down here in the land of the free.
Let's stop all the insanity.

You ask me about the candidates,
I'll tell you how they all should rate.
Don't look at their morals, just focus on issues.
Stop whining, complaining, get rid of your tissues.
If you want to change this country's ways,
Then don't move out. Let's discuss future days,
To make positive change, so you can stay.

So who is to say what's right and what's wrong?
If you have an opinion, then write a song.
We're what we are. What? We are who we are.
Though some are not able, all reach for the stars.

Limerick

I wanted to write a limerick,
But I can't find a rhyme
For limerick!
The heck with it!

Elie Wiesel

This is a poem about Elie Wiesel,
Who survived Nazi terror,
But had peaceful reprisal.
He was a friend to one and all.
A man of peace, he heeded the call.
Eternity spoke through his human mouth.
He was known in the east, west, north and south.
He spoke with gravity,
For he survived the depravity.

He said, "Think higher. Live deeper."
He was no liar. He was a keeper.
He spoke for millions, slaughtered in war,
And those who had no voice before,
While wondering what war's point was for.
He blessed us with history come alive,
And gave us a goal for which we should strive.
He reminded us all to never forget,
And his words will go on and on, I bet.

Flowers

Violets are blue,
Roses are red.
I can't get you
Out of my head!

The Living And The Dead

Gravestones mark the lives of the dead,
But so do the memories inside your head.
Some die by accident.
We all die when our lives are spent.
Some die in a war.
You wonder what some are living for.
Some just die from ripe old age.
Some die in peace, some die in rage.
Some die of a fatal disease.
Some die trying, but never please.
All who die are important to some.
Eventually you will be that one.

I'm fortunate to have family and friends,
But I don't know how my life will end.
I'd like to die in my sleep, at peace,
Or surrounded by family and friends when I cease.
But while I'm alive, I'll fight to strive,
As life is a test which no one survives.
I'm sure that many have regrets.
All hope their loved ones don't forget.
I hope your illusion I don't shatter,
But the truth, you must know,
Is that all lives matter.

Conglomerate

We're run by a conglomerate.
The truth, they do not honor it.
Magazines, books and papers you choose,
To find out what's happening in the news,
The radio, movies and TV,
They all lie to you. They all lie to me.

Conglomerate spits out junk and trash.
It's all about the money, the cash.
Our world can be suddenly gone in a flash.
The truth is still censored on TV,
In the land of the brave and home of the free,
At every opportunity.

They control social issues and politics.
They have their agenda and they want it to stick.
Millions are lied to, millions controlled,
Destroying our very lives and souls.

Conglomerate says it doesn't exist,
But those rumors persist and persist.

Conglomerate offers you crooks and jerks,
But no solutions that really work.
Conglomerate focuses on latest sensations,
While misleading a trusting nation.
Conglomerate focuses on the rich and wealthy,
While hiding the truth with techniques stealthy.

Everyone watches the Kardashians,
While the self-absorbed follow passions.
Commercials focus on drugs, cars and fashions,
Distracting us from true actions.
A few seek wisdom of the ages,
Not fooled by singers on the stages,
While some seek guidance from prophets and sages.

Now there's a voice out there that tells the truth,
To share with each other and your youths.
Conglomerate ignores it or tells it in blurbs.
No wonder our society's disturbed.
Conglomerate and the government lies,
As every nation sends out its spies.

The truth can help improve your life,
And overcome all the rage and strife.
There are two sides to every story.
You won't find it in the conglomerate's glory.

The people want happiness and success.
Conglomerate acts in self-interest.
But there is still hope for a world in balance,
Where all people can utilize their talents.

While many watch reality shows,
There's a small group of people that really know.

The truth is out there, fleet and quick.
You have to discuss it. Then it will stick.
Blogs, articles, grassroots and internet,
Are out there to help us, so don't forget.
Citizens, filmmakers and newspapers,
Honest sources tell truth about capers.

We're the least informed and the most entertained.
Not knowing the truth is causing us pain.
Conglomerate spreads feelings of lack and fear,
But if you look closely, the truth is near.
Conglomerate says how to think and act,
But it's time to take our country back,
From big business, the media, political hacks.
Take part and learn and think for yourself,
In the fight against power and gargantuan wealth.

The world needs thinkers and leaders of change,
To take the truth and rearrange,
To take the knowledge that is forbidden,
And reveal the news conglomerate's hidden.
By changing our thoughts, we change what is real.
We are responsible for how we feel.

What's Really Going On

There was a man named Marvin Gaye,
Who wrote a song and sang it his way.
The song he wrote applies today.

When you turn your radio on,
I hope that you will hear this song.
I'll make my point, but not too long.
I'm warning you now, this message is strong.

This war on the streets is not about race,
About the color of skin on a face.
It's not about uniformed men of blue.
Listen to me, and I'll tell you what's true.

This thing about race is a screen of smoke.
Stop yelling and listen, this is no joke.
It's really class warfare fought on the street,
And frustrations of those that can't compete.
It's really a war 'tween haves and have nots.
The rich want more than they've already got.

Opportunity's door isn't there for the poor.
The rich want to push them down on the floor.
When black kills white or white kills black,
The media covers those attacks.
When black kills black or poor kills poor,
The media chooses to ignore,
But this is what happens so much more.

Again, it's a war between the classes.
Both sides want to kick some asses.
Now it's time to heal our hateful past,
So the greatness of this country lasts.
It better happen, and happen fast.

Both sides have got to stop all the killing.
Just listen to me, take heed and be willing.

Dancing With Fruit

I'd like to waltz in New Paultz.
I'd like to tango while eating a mango.
I'd like to jitterbug then give the girl a hug.

Your Purpose

I don't want to make you nervous.
I'll show you how to find your purpose.

People come into your life,
At times of joy and times of strife.
They are there for a reason,
Some for a lifetime, some for a season.

Life presents its panoply,
For you to choose and you to see.

You feel a peace though you are nervous,
You sense that you have found your purpose.

You have some pop. You have vitality,
To turn your dreams into reality.

You overcome your trials with ease,
Surrounded by a feeling of peace.

It comes to you in a flash of light.
You know your reasons to win the fight.

So now you know the way to go.
Heed my advice, but take it slow.

Jersey's Okay With Me

When I was young, I hated this state.
I did everything to get away from it.
But now I think it really rates.
When I was a kid, I'd run and hide,
But now I've got that Jersey Pride.

We've had many people of note,
Politicians for whom I'd vote,
Like Wilson and Cory Booker and Christie.
When I think of them, my eyes get misty.

At the well near Freehold was Molly Pitcher.
We all get along, whether poorer or richer.
Am I painting an accurate picture?
In the past, there was Thomas Edison.
Now Jersey makes high tech and medicine.

Frank Sinatra did it his way.
On the Turnpike and Parkway, you pay, pay, pay.
The Jersey Shore's great for summer days.

We have Yankee of note, mister Yogi Berra.
I can't think of a state that's fairer.

A man on the moon was an Aldrin named Buzz.
We're proud of what our Jerseyans do.
We're the home of Bruce Springsteen, "The Boss."
Without his songs, we'd be at a loss.

Southside Johnny and The Asbury Jukes!
Put down this state and it makes me puke.

Then, of course, there is Bon Jovi.
We're so packed with people, it's hard to be lonely.
I'll tell you the truth, right down to the marrow,
Some of us even like Tony Soprano.

Some think this state's filled with crooks and scams,
But the Jersey Devil is our only scam.
We all like our pork roll and Taylor ham.
We raise tomatoes, corn and blueberries, too.
Good food for me and good food for you.

Now we've got Jersey winters and summer heat.
Some of us live in the county seat.
Our salt water taffy is salty and sweet.
Don't tell us that we can't compete.
In the north, they like Yanks, Jets and Giants.
The Phillies and Eagles, in the south, they're reliant.

Welcome to Jersey, now please go home.
This is the land where Jerseyans roam.
The rest of this country can leave us alone.
So this is Jersey, both good and bad.
Put this state down, and it makes me mad.

Now I've lived in several other states,
Some were okay, but none were so great,
As my home, New Jersey, the Garden State.
It's plain to note, and easy to see,
That Jersey's okay. It's okay with me.

What I Am

I never was a butcher.
I never was a baker.
I never really was
A mover or a shaker,
But one thing I am,
Is a poetry maker.

A Question

Did it ever cross your mind to think
That some cops are sad?
They have feelings, too,
And they witness the bad.

One man in blue
Was overdue.
To his head he put a gun.
He wanted his life to be done.
He thought of his wife.
Her name was Marge.
He decided to put himself in charge.
He called another man in blue,
Whose dedication was honest and true.
He got help with his mental health.

Cops put their life on the line,
For not much wealth.
More cops die of suicide,
Than anything else.

For the pain they face each day on the job,
It's so sad, it makes me sob.

Is this what it's come to,
In this day and age,
Where cops on the street
Face daily rage?
Do you know what to do,
At this nation's stage,
Where the streets are filled
With anger and rage?

Liv

I live for Liv,
Who works in a bar.
She works very hard,
In my eyes she's a star.
If I had a car,
I'd take her near and far.

She's my hero.
She's my reason for living.
If she makes a mistake,
I am always forgiving.
She's the light of my life.
She'll be someone's wife.

I live for Liv,
Who works in a bar.
She works very hard.
In my eyes she's a star.

If I had a car,
I'd take her near and far.

In the world that we live in,
You're a fortunate soul,
If you have someone to share your life,
And set mutual goals,
In a world so disrupted
And out of control.

I live for Liv,
Who works in a bar.
She works very hard.
In my eyes she's a star.
If I had a car,
I'd take her near and far.

Look at the sky
When the stars are a-shining.
She stands out in a crowd.
You know I'm not lying.
We do so much talking,
It's a good thing I'm walking.

Nature

I've taken a liking to lichen.
I'm rather fond of a pond.
If I had a wish,
I'd wish for a fish,
And I'd like to see a tree,

But most importantly,
I'll see humanity,
In both you and me.

Television

I've seen The Talk, The Chew
And The View.
It seems to me that there's nothing new.
When it comes to TV, what can we do?
When it comes to Comcast,
We all are screwed.

A Poem For You

How was I to know,
That day so long ago,
When you came into my life,
And soon became my wife?
But none I wrote for you.
I'm shamed that I did not.
You know it and it's true.

Sickness

Doctor, doctor,
I seem to be ill.
Can I find the cure in a pill?

Are there any lotions, potions or notions
That can cure my many ills?

Doctor my eyes just burn in pain,
And the memory of her remains,
Though I know that I will never have
Her to act as a healing salve.

I don't want to start a commotion,
But I've got problems with my emotions.
I'm feeling sad. It hurts so bad.
Can you give me something so I feel glad?

In this world of pain and gloom,
Just keep me out of the emergency room.
Is that a nurse I see?
Can you introduce her to me?

The Rich And The Poor

The rich are the rich,
The poor are the poor,
But most are caught in the middle.
So stay in school,
Obey all the rules,
And learn how to play the fiddle!

Poe's Bird

Poe had a bird,
Or so I heard.
I think it was a raven.

I read it once or twice, I know,
When 'ere I had the craving.

Days Of The Week

Sunday comes,
The week begins.
Some go to church
To atone for their sins.
It is time for family dinners.
Once again, we all are sinners.
We all root for our favorite teams.
It's just a sport,
But we go to extremes.

Monday comes.
To school or work,
To learn to become a cog in a wheel,
Regardless of what we think or feel.

Tuesday comes,
Another day,
To live your life
In your own way.

Wednesday's here.

It's hump day, all!
In winter, spring, summer and fall.

Thursday's here.
We celebrate!
Whether alone, or on a date.

Friday again,
More of the same.
We all go out and play our games.

Saturday comes,
Another week ends.
We spend it all
With family and friends.

Where Is God?

Where is God in outer space,
To see this tired and troubled place?
So full of war and poverty,
And He talks of eternity.

Living in the inner city,
Without money, without pity.
Facing drugs and ignorance,
It doesn't make too much sense.

The child without arms or legs,
Is treated like unholy dregs.
The drunkard drinks kegs of beer,
To conquer his legitimate fears.

So where is God in all of this?
Am I wrong or just amiss?
If I'm wrong, just show me this.

For My Children

I didn't do enough for you.
That's why life was rough for you.
I was high and mighty in my chair,
But I wasn't with you there,
So life for you just wasn't fair.
I'm ashamed that you had such a scare.
I should have been there.
Should have been there.

When people do commiserate,
They talk about how much they hate.
All I cared about were dates,
While you were suffering,
And while I sought the golden ring,
You lost everything.
What am I now?
A loser, large.
I never really was in charge.

For Her

I've got your turtle, painting and book.
I like to steal a furtive look,
While you flirt
With someone too old.

I hope that I am not too bold,
But as this story does unfold,
I'd like to say,
In a special way,
That maybe, just maybe,
Some future day –
We might be relatives.

Love

HOW can I write about love?
How can I WRITE about love?
How can I write about LOVE?

How can I not?

Crescent Moon

I look up at the crescent moon,
And think about better times,
Like June.

In the sky I also see Venus.
I can figure it out,
It takes no genius.

You've fallen for another man.
You've deviated from our plan,
And left me all alone,

Wondering
If the magic
Will ever happen again.

Drip

I hear the drip, drip, drip of my shower.
Every day. Every minute. Every hour.
When I'm lying in my bed,
It keeps pounding in my head!
Maybe I should plant a flower.

Veterans Day

Today, we celebrate Veterans Day,
For all the soldiers of the USA.
Especially in World War Two,
WE knew just what we had to do.

Allied heroes one and heroes all,
The dreaded Nazis had to fall.
They wanted to ban the Jewish race
From Europe and this earthly place.

We came from the west, we came from the east,
To defeat the mark of the beast.
Heroes like Patton and Eisenhower
Brought about Hitler's final hour.

The focus then was on Japan,
The land of the rising sun.

A couple of bombs never used before
Brought about the end of the war.

So here's to heroes, including my dad –
The greatest generation we ever had!

Months Of The Year

January begins the year.
Some start it with joy,
Some start it with fear.
Some start it by shedding a little tear.
Snow is not measured in inches, but feet.
All the kids that miss school
Think it's pretty neat!
There's even a day in this month
For a King,
Who changed civil rights
And everything.

February brings more snow.
On the fourteenth,
Hearts burn with a glow.

March is the war between
Winter and spring,
With snow and ice and rain and sunshine.
Don't worry folks, all will be fine.

The flowers of May come from April showers,
So don't worry if it pours for hours.

May's an important month, for sure.
It's my birthday that opened my door.

June is the month for many a bride,
And grooms that look at them with pride.

July has Independence Day.
The world's greatest country
Is the USA!

August brings the dog days of summer.
If your faucet breaks, just call a plumber.

September is time for new school clothes,
So you sit at your desks, in rows upon rows.
At night, we watch the new TV shows,
With stars and actors we all love and know.
And finally, there are the new cars.
On streets and roads, they'll take us so far.

October is time for cavities and candy.
Dentists think it's fine and dandy.

November is football and Thanksgiving Day.
We've got much to be thankful for,
In our own way.

December brings Christmas,
The birth of our Lord,
As we all fight for presents
We all can't afford.

A Block Away

Allison, a block away –
You thought you taught
Me how to pray.
But my life was a giveaway.

Two directions, far apart –
We both followed our own heart.
Yours rated G, mine rated R.
You were the best.
I was never a star.

My Mind

My mind drifts like the snow.
I don't always know where
It's going to go.

Mariposa

You came into my life like a mariposa.
You are the manzana of my eye.
I look into your eyes of azul.

It would truly break my Corazon,
If you left me all alone.
It would make me look like a fool.

I think back of the women I have known,
In the times that I'm alone,
And wonder where I went wrong.

So now I sit here, writing a song,
Not too short and not too long.
Maybe they'll play it on the radio.

Fame and fortune will set me free,
And open opportunities,
But Spanish is too hard for me!

Money

Poems, essays and screenplays –
These are my money-making ways.

Birth

I hear the thump of my mother's heart.
I think I am about to start.
Whoosh! Swoosh!
It is a flood!
Is that red stuff what's called blood?
What is that blinding light I see?
Oh yes, it is the birth of me!

Bruce

He infused your soul
With rock and roll.
He was a scrawny kid from Jersey.
But when he played that guitar,
You knew he'd go far,
For he played it without mercy.

He was born to run in the USA.
His songs were like anthems
We wanted to pray.
In nineteen fifty-seven he saw the king.
That little taste of heaven was the beginning.

In seventy-one they started calling him "Boss."
If he had died, it would have been a loss.
He could do no wrong and he wrote songs
About the rock and roll,
The power and glory.
It's all here,
In Springsteen's story.

"What time is it?" I said,
As I looked at the clock,
"It's time to go
To the First Church of Rock!"

Tulip

I see your red tulip.
I see your two red lips.
I can see the curve of your hips.
I feel the touch of your fingertips.

Beauty

Beauty is only skin deep,
But ugly is right down to the bone.
If I can't spend my life with a beauty,
I'd rather be alone.

Conflict

In a conflict between nations,
Do you have good information?
Do you have a resolution?
Do you have a good solution,
In the course of evolution?

My Wife

I love the beauty of Marilyn Monroe,
And Kelly Stables from some old show.
I love the beauty of Mariah Carey,
But I think she married some guy named Gary.

And then there's the gorgeous Jessica Simpson.
I don't have a rhyme for her.
But of all the beauties I've seen
In my life,
None are so beautiful
As my wife.

Untitled

If you have hope,
It can help you cope,
In your desperate, lonely hours.
Empowerment is heaven sent,
And blooms just like the flowers.
So if you have a choice,
Just raise your voice!

Justin Case

Justin Case
Is the name to my face,
So please, mister bouncer,
Let me into this place!

Mis Led

Mis led.
Force fed.
Brain dead.

After The Shower

I itch.
I itch.
The itch remains.
What can I say?
Oh, what a pain!

Scratch

I need scratch!
I need scratch!
That's because I'm short on cash!

Shingles

You just got a shot
For shingles.
If you're single, you can mingle,
Or, you can snack on some Pringles.

Jesus Wept

Jesus wept when Lazarus died,
Until He came upon his side.
When Lazarus rose up from the dead,
It was a symbol
Of those that Christ would wed.

"Jesus wept," the shortest verse,
To overcome Satan's sinful curse.

Wedding Day

I bought a suit in charcoal gray,
For my daughter's wedding day.
I bought two shirts – one white, one pink.
Now I'm on the financial brink.
I bought two shirts – one pink, one white.
Now my money's really tight.

I also bought two red ties.
I hope the wedding turns out nice.

Eagles Quarterback

He came and Wentz.
Money that he's paid
Is money well spent.
Boy, those Eagles fans
Sure are intense!

Might I be so bold
As to predict
Nick Foles
Will take them to
The Superbowl?

Silent Protest

Quiet!

That's it!

Dysfunctional

Dysfunctional.
Getting drunk, and all.
Getting stoned.
Smoking a bone.
All together,
Yet all alone.

Night

When I go to sleep at night,
I think of who I'll cuddle tight.
I think of you.
It's true.
It's what I want to do.

I want to hold you in a spoon,
As we sleep beneath the moon.
I hope you think I'm not a goon.

Countries

Greenland isn't green –
At least, not in the pictures
That I've seen.

Iceland isn't all ice –
Although I hear it's very nice.

Turkey, Greece and Hungary
All share in Europe's border.
Go to a diner,
And that's quite a tall order.

Regression

Adults sucking on lollipops.
When it comes to candy,

They're the tops.

Go to Dunkin' Donuts
And fill it up –
Coffee in an oversized sippy cup.

Go to Barnes and Noble
And take a look –
Now they have adult coloring books.

Star Trek

If you're the first among the crew
To beam down,
You know you're doomed.

Odd Couple

Felix and Oscar are quite the pair,
In the apartment that they share.
If on their feet they get some blisters,

They can double date
With the Pidgeon sisters.

Al Bundy

My name is Al Bundy,
And I hate Mondays.
I sell shoes,
But this is no news.
All the fat women give me abuse.
I do it all for a few dollars a day,
But I deserve a raise in pay.

Inauguration Day

Today is Inauguration Day,
Where we gather together, unite and pray.
For our enemies, like Russia and China
Do not want to play.

Heaven

Four, seven, eight.
Tour heaven late.

Drinking

I would like to tie one on,
In Taiwon.

Clothing

I would like to wear a hat
In Cape Hatteras.
I would like to wear some glasses
While hiking through some mountain passes.
I would like to have a beard
While sailing around Cape Fear.
I would like a London Fog
While walking through London's fog.
I would like to wear a suit
As I walk through Beirut.
I would like to wear some pants
As I travel through France.
I would like to wear some shoes
As I travel through Peru.

Cars Two

I'd like to drive an Aston Martin
To go and visit Dolly Parton.
I'd like to drive a Buick,
Or maybe I won't want to do it.
I'd like to drive a Chevy,
But only if it's not too heavy.
I'd like to drive a Dodge
To a mountain lodge.
I'd like to drive a Mustang Ford,
I know that I will not get bored.
I'd like to drive a Honda,
But only if I meet Jane Fonda.
I'd like to drive a Jaguar,

But only if it's not too far.
I'd like to drive a Kia
To see the show, Momma Mia.
I'd like to drive a Lotus
To see the POTUS.
I'd like to drive a Mercury,
If it's not too jerkury.
I'd like to drive a Neon
To see my good friend, Leon.
I'd like to drive a Porshe,
Of coursha.
I'd like to drive a Rolls Royce.
It would be my car of choice.
I'd like to drive a Volvo,
But only if it's safe and slow.
I'd like to drive a Willys,
If it doesn't give me the willies.
I'd like to drive a Yugo.
Oh, forget about it – you know.
I'd like to drive a Z,
But only if it's free.
I can't find a rhyme for X.
I'm perplexed.
I'd like to drive a Mini Cooper,
But only if there are no troopers.

Sty

If you have a sty
In your eye,
Go to the doctor,
Who is a good guy.
When you come home,

You can have some pie.
If you go on vacation,
You ought to fly.

Or go see a movie with Stallone,
Nicknamed Sly.

Angels

How many angels are on the head of a pin?
No matter what I do, I just can't win.
Why do I watch this show or that show on TV?
As if I'm getting my cable for free.
Do I have to put up with this for eternity?
Why do people always have to judge?
I think it's because they are
Holding a grudge.

Creativity

Creativity.
It's always within me,
For my poetry.

Claustrophobia

Walls pushing in,
Consistently,
Like a flood.

Squirrels

Squirrels are hairy creatures.
They have such hairy features.

Thinking Of Her

I think of her,
Lying in my bed.
I think of her so often,
I can't get her out of my head.
I want to cuddle her,
And hold her like a spoon,
And feel the warmth of her body,
With the rising of the moon.

Prolific

They say I'm prolific,
And that's terrific,
Because I try and try,
But what's to become
Of all that I've done,
When I pass away and die?

Silence

Is silence deadly, or golden?
Does it make you shy, or heady, or embolden?

Forgotten Man

Hey!
It's me!
Have you forgotten me?
Mister politician.
In the home of the free?
While I am enslaved in poverty?
You fly above it all,
While we crawl.

Valentine's Day

I know it isn't Valentine's Day,
But I love you, anyway.
Will you marry me?

Rutgers

The Rutgers football team looks good.
They're all wearing their new jerseys.
I'm playing on the other team,
So Rutgers, please don't hurt me.

I'll Wait

I'll wait.
I'll wait.
I'll wait, dear, for your answer,
But at our wedding reception,
We will not be the dancers.

After This World

After this world,
What will be?
Memories of you and me?
Will we branch out like the old oak tree?
Or will there be nothing?

Dress For The Mess

Long before you dress for success,
You must dress –
Yes, dress for the mess.
I'm talking about the rain and snow.
I know it's a pain,
But you've got to go.
On top of your shoes, wear some galoshes.
Bring some nice snacks, and some nice gnoshes.

If you're a lucky girl or fella,
You can bring along an umbrella.

Printed in the United States
By Bookmasters